a taste of morocco

a taste of
morocco

CLARE FERGUSON

with photography by PETER CASSIDY

jacqui
small

First published in 2007 by Jacqui Small LLP
an imprint of Aurum Press Ltd
7 Greenland Street
London NW1 0ND

Publisher   Jacqui Small
Editorial Manager   Judith Hannam
Editor   Madeline Weston
Art Director   Ashley Western
Photography   Peter Cassidy
Stylist   Roisin Nield
Food stylist   Clare Ferguson
Assistant Food stylist   Debbie Dalgliesh
Production   Peter Colley

ISBN-10: 1 903221 79 X
ISBN-13: 978 1 903221 79 2

2010   2009   2008   2007

10 9 8 7 6 5 4 3 2 1

Printed in China

Half title page, Keneffa, see page 62.
Title page, King Prawn Brochettes, see page 32.
Contents page, Lettuce and Purslane Salad with Orange, see page 17.

contents

introduction and basic ingredients

Introduction

Morocco is a glorious adventure waiting to happen to any keen traveller and every discerning cook.

This splendid country in north-western Africa is blessed with rich resources and a vibrant food culture reflecting a grand imperialist past and a wealth of influences absorbed over the centuries from its many traders, invaders and conquering powers.

Arab, Phoenician, Senegalese, Sudanese, Spanish, Portuguese, Middle Eastern and, in particular, French cuisine can be traced throughout its dishes, but the indigenous Berber peoples of Morocco have absorbed and adapted these trends in an inimitable way: the food is distinct, pungent, seasonal and intensely regional.

Brilliant sunshine, adequate rainfall, large swathes of fertile agricultural land, desert oases, mountain ranges, rivers and fish-rich coastlines combine to create produce of great distinctiveness from pomegranates to pigeons.

Some unique products: couscous, s'men, argan oil, the herb za'atar, ouarka pastry and preserved lemons add excitement and interest. Learning how to use and enjoy these will enrich your skills and knowledge; broaden your palate.

Moroccan hospitality is legendary: family meals often extend to include friends, neighbours, and outsiders with grace, style and good humour. Generosity is part of the way of life here.

Good food and drink are celebrated: these sustain both body and spirit and the rituals of the table are relished. This book offers a taste of a fascinating country.

Spices, Herbs, Aromatics

1 CELERY LEAF. These luminous green leaves are chopped into fresh and cooked herb mixes as well as being used in soups, stuffings, tagines and as flavourings for kefta. The stems. too, are popularly used.

2 THYME. *Thymus vulgaris*, with its tiny green pungent leaves, both antiseptic and preservative, is the best alternative if no *za'atar* is available.

3 ONIONS, called *sla*, are integral to Moroccan cooking. Fat bunches of salad onion abound in every market and are used often. Large tawny Spanish type onions and glossy red onions also star in many dishes, both raw and cooked.

4 ANISE SEEDS or Aniseed, known as *nafaa* or *habbt hlawa*, are small, green-gold seeds with a hot, liquorice-anise taste. Excellent with fish, it is delicious in and on breads. (If unobtainable, use dill or fennel seeds, or even caraway, similar but not identical.)

5 GUM MASTIC. These whitish granules (called *niska*), crushed, yield an intense, resinous, warm fragrance which flatters almond pastes, certain iced desserts and custards; even some savoury dishes. Gum mastic comes from the lentisc bush. Small 'discs' of the ripe resin form and solidify. Grind it using a pestle and mortar or spice grinder with some coarse sugar. Musk, gum Arabic and gum tragacanth are very different and often confused with gum mastic.

6 ZA'ATAR. *Originum cyriacum*, an intense, peppery herb with a taste and smell like a mix of thyme-oregano-marjoram, is hard to find outside Morocco's Mediterranean regions, except dried. Fresh thyme mixed with oregano or marjoram and a pinch of pepper makes a good alternative.

Confusingly it has nothing at all to do with the thyme-sumac-sesame mix called *zahtar* from stores stocking Middle Eastern spices.

7 PAPRIKA. Known as *felfla hlouwa*, this fragrant, red powder often excels in tomato-based tagines, sauces, stews or brochettes. It can be scarlet or crimson. Check intensity and taste before buying.

8 CUMIN, called *kamoon* in Morocco, is a distinguishing taste of Morocco. Flaky salt and freshly ground cumin may be condiments offered at the table. Toasted briefly, to dry it, the seeds are then ground: refreshingly pungent. Its digestive properties are stressed. Essential in many kefta, seafood, poultry and game dishes, brochettes and certain salads.

9 TURMERIC. This tropical root *quekoum*, related to the ginger family, has a pungent, bitter flavour and colours foods a greenish yellow (unlike saffron's warm clarity). Buy the small, dried roots and grind them, or buy this spice in powder form, testing for pungency first. Harira soup always contains this spice.

10 HONEY DATES. *Rhamnus zizphys*, called *nabka* in Morocco, is a small, shiny, red-brown fruity seasoning, not unlike a tiny cherry with an inedible stone. Dried, these provide sweet-sharp accents in tagines and certain meat stews. Substitute? Try a splash of pomegranate or lemon juice.

11 SAFFRON. Called *zafrane*, these precious stigma of the *crocus sativus* plant grown in Morocco are claimed to surpass the Spanish variety. The deep orange-crimson strands yield a superb fragrance and warm yellow colour once ground then dissolved in one of the liquid ingredients of the dish. Egg, seafood, poultry and game dishes benefit from it. Moroccan cooks may mix it with a tasteless yellow pigment, or turmeric, for cheapness: not ideal. In celebratory dishes add it late in the cooking for the best effects.

12 CAYENNE. *Felfla soudaniya* is the Moroccan name, reflecting its Senegalese links. Pale orange-yellow and fiercely hot, it is used, often with milder pepper flavours such as paprika, in most dishes: stews, grain dishes, pastries, brochettes, stuffings, sauces. (*Felfla harra*, a sharp, hot peppery mix, is made from cayenne, paprika and long peppers: useful in stuffed breads and snacks.)

13 PEPPERCORNS, black, are called *el beza*. Added whole, crushed or ground, these are often added early in cooking. Black pepper is often combined with ginger and cayenne or paprika. Long pepper, *piper longum*, tasting similar, has Asian origins.

14 CHILLI. Dried, these range from orange to crimson; from tiny to large. They may be broken into flakes, or added whole or lightly crushed to recipes for a boost of flavour.

15 CASSIA AND CINNAMON. Both scrolled, tawny sticks of cinnamon (*dar el cini*) and the coarser-looking shards of cassia (*karfa*) are essentials, in both sweet and savoury dishes. Cinnamon is more delicate; cassia has a more robust flavour and is used more often, ground into powder and whole. Harira soup, *b'stilla*, kefta, dessert rice, couscous and spiced coffee all use cassia or cinnamon.

16 S'MEN (also pronounced as *samen, sman, semneh,* or *sminn*) is the traditional cooking fat most commonly used and prized in Moroccan cuisine. Made from the milk of sheep or goats, this butter is spiced, cooked at a high temperature, salted and strained. The resulting liquid will then be aged, often in sealed containers buried in the ground. It is similar to ghee but has a more cheese-like, sharp flavour. S'men has great cultural significance. It may be used as a token of respect to honour guests. Innovative Moroccan chefs substitute butter or ghee instead of s'men, adding Parmesan for cheesy savouriness.

17 OLIVES. Magnificent displays of these enliven every souk, every store. Snack foods

and seasonings, olives enhance countless soups, tagines, purées, breads. Two main categories exist: hard, green-ripe cracked olives, beaten after brining, are again salt-immersed until mellow. Garlic, citrus and fennel or bay are usual additions. Mid-ripe, rainbow-hued olives, the other category, are plump, ripe, usually brined; often mellowed in olive oil and fresh lemon juice at home.

18 HONEY. Thick, dark crystallized mountain honey is prized, distinctive, used raw and in certain cakes, pastries and sweetmeats. Clear liquid honeys, often floral-fragranced enhance breakfast, or are used as glazes.

19 GARLIC, called *tourma*, is often found as small white or pink bulbs, often bunched. Used profusely in savoury dishes raw and cooked, but it even features, with honey, in certain sweet dishes. Fresh and dried, this is a culinary essential.

20 GINGER. Called *kinjbir*, this, either as dried, small, hard roots or powder, is a fragrant peppery and reviving taste in tagines, makalli dishes. With black pepper it becomes a seasoning. Used little in sweet dishes, it is sold less often fresh than dried.

21 DATES. Fresh, apple-crisp dates, still on the branch – also dried, sticky, close-packed dates – are favoured fruits cum sweetmeats. 'Deglet nour' (page 7) are typical examples, sold here and in Tunisia.

22 SUGAR LUMPS. Valued as a sweetener for tea and in many desserts, preserves and candies, lumps are often pounded with aromatics, for use as seasonings. Granulated, caster, icing sugar and vanilla sugar are popularly utilized.

ORANGE FLOWER WATER (*zhaat*) and ROSE WATER (*mai ward*). These fragrant waters are made using massive volumes of aromatic flowers (Bergamot orange blossoms and rosebuds) using *alembic* or *quettara* stills. They have astonishing intensity of scent and taste; perfect in cooking and flavouring. Buy authentic French, Lebanese or Middle Eastern products. Triple-distilled are especially fine.

KHELEA (beef confit). This tasty preserved beef in strips, is a snack food and flavouring in tagines, omelettes, stews. In Morocco it is air-dried over several days after salting and spicing with cumin and coriander. Then it is heated and sealed in beef dripping and/or olive oil, in which it is matured. Removed using tongs, the beef 'confit' is cut up then paired with bread, pickles, olives and in egg dishes.

PRESERVED LEMONS. Salt-cured lemons are an essential taste in many savoury Moroccan dishes. The pulp is sometimes discarded; the skin and pith is the active seasoning (see page 43). Avoid store-bought preserved lemons: preservatives give these an unpleasant taste.

HARISSA PASTE. This vividly potent spicy red condiment is made from hot red chillies cooked with red capsicum and/or carrots, then seasoned with salt, ground coriander, cumin and caraway seeds, and puréed to a rough paste. French and North African grocers and delis stock this. Common in Tunisia and Algeria, it is also used extensively in Morocco, especially with couscous, rice etc.

OUARKA (*feuilles de brick*) pastry) and equivalents. *Ouarka* (*warka*) are fine, thin, round pancake pastry 'leaves' which, folded or in layers, go to create many dishes including the famous *b'stilla* (*pastille*) pies, also *briouats* (*briwats*) made in triangles, cornets and rectangles.

Delicious deep-fried, this pastry is less good baked: so the best alternative is Greek filo (phyllo) pastry, but strudel pastry or even spring roll pastry may also be substituted.

ARGAN OIL. A product uniquely Moroccan, with a nutty, earthy, toasty flavour. Goats avidly devour the little yellow fruits of the Argan trees. Once they excrete the stones, the nuts (kernels) are extracted, processed and pressed to yield a 'naturally aged' oil: it is an acquired taste; expensive, even in Morocco. Smell and taste before you buy. Avoid reddish-coloured massage oils: they are non culinary.

BREADS. Loaves of all shapes are all popular, made from wheat flour, wholegrain flours, semolina flour or a mix of these; also

from maize, barley and rye flours. Sesame and aniseed add interest. In past times the communal oven was used to bake the family's breads. Even today this remains the popular choice for daily baking. In courtyards of large *riads* (houses) outdoor conical clay ovens called *tannouts* are still used to cook flatbreads. The breads are slapped onto the heated inner walls; cooked, they fall into the ashes. Breads are also cooked on domed or flat griddles or tagines. In souks vendors sell spongy *beghrir* breads (see page 58), also spicy, pastry-bread 'pizzas' (see page 55): delicious, fresh and hot.

COUSCOUS. This is the Moroccan national dish. Its name means both the grain itself and the dish of which it is a part. Poultry, meat, game, fish cook in the base of a couscoussier (a metal pan with a steamer and lid above) with stock, aromatics, herbs, vegetables. Above it the grains steam. Couscous is semolina, the central part of durum wheat grains, which have been ground, moistened, flour-dusted ('rolled') then steamed until fluffy and light.

Couscous is favoured for celebrations and laments; eaten towards the end of the feast to ensure no one goes hungry; eaten as a dessert. Muslim families traditionally eat couscous together each Friday, their holy day. In past times, Moroccan families took their own wheat to be milled.

Combine 500g (1lb 2oz) 'moyen' (medium grade) couscous with 600ml (2¾ cups) hand-hot, salted water. Stir, leave 8 minutes to plump up; add 2 tablespoons superb olive oil. Stir; plump up again. Oven-cook, covered, at 200°C (400°F) for 20 minutes. Add s'men or ghee. Fluff again. Serve. (Alternatively microwave cook on High in three 2 minute bursts.)

OTHER ESSENTIAL MOROCCAN CULINARIES

Fresh parsley (*madnouss*), fresh mint (*nana*), and fresh coriander (cilantro)(*kosbour*) are considered the Moroccan 'herb trinity'. Allspice, cloves, fenugreek, frankincense, orris root, pomegranate molasses, lavender, liquorice twigs, nutmeg, rosepetals, verbena also *ras el hanout* (page 46) are all very important flavourings.

TOP ROW
Orange flower water; rose water; mint tea

MIDDLE ROW
Khelea beef confit; wheat couscous (top)
and barley couscous (bottom); preserved lemons

BOTTOM ROW
Harissa paste; ouarka pastry sheets (*feuilles de brick*); argan oil

appetizers, salads, vegetables and soups

aubergine salad with coriander and yoghurt

Aubergines (eggplants) are found in every souk. Cooked to a soft sweetness they are the mainstay of many stews, tagines and dishes such as couscous. I tasted this delicious salad, warm, inside a piece of *khubz* bread in a tiny café in the Marrakesh medina.

1 Push the point of a paring knife blade into each aubergine (eggplant) in 4 places. Push the garlic slivers into the cuts.

2 Spear each aubergine (eggplant) between two sturdy forks and cook directly over a high gas flame, turning it regularly until the outside is evenly charred, the smell aromatic and the inner pulp feels soft – about 8–12 minutes each. (If preferred, chargrill on a rack over charcoal for a slightly longer time or bake at 250ºC (500ºF) on top rack of oven for about 35 minutes.)

3 Once the aubergines (eggplants) cool, peel and discard most of the skin. Set the flesh in a sieve. Press gently to drain off some of the juices. Discard these.

4 Mash, pound or use a hand-held food mill to reduce the flesh to a rough purée. Stir in the spices and olive oil. Taste: add juice to season.

5 Pile the purée into a serving dish. Swirl some yoghurt on top. Scatter some coriander (cilantro) leaves over. Serve warm or cool with some flatbreads.

SERVES 4–6 (MAKES 550g)

900g (2 or 3 medium–large) aubergines (eggplants), stems intact
6 garlic cloves, halved lengthwise
1 teaspoon each paprika, cumin seeds and coriander seeds, freshly ground together
2 tablespoons extra-virgin olive oil
2 tablespoons freshly squeezed lime or lemon juice

TO GARNISH
2 tablespoons natural yoghurt or buttermilk
small handful fresh coriander (cilantro) leaves

TO SERVE
flatbreads, warmed

mammounia tomates confites

During my stay in Marrakesh, the famed *La Mammounia Hotel* was closed. I am assured by an aficionado that this tomato recipe is one of their most fêted dishes. The saffron and added sweetness give a quaint perfumed twist to an old favourite.

1 Scoop out the pulp from each tomato half but leave in the ribs. (Reserve the pulp: use it in soups or sauces.)

2 Put two pinches of the saffron with the sugar, salt, cinnamon, into a mortar and grind using a pestle or grind using an electric spice grinder to a powder.

3 Oil a large, shallow, ovenproof dish. Set the tomato halves on it. Scatter the spiced seasoning over the half tomatoes, then drizzle the remaining olive oil and the orange flower water over. Scatter the remaining saffron over.

4 Bake at 110ºC (225ºF) for 3–4 hours, if time allows. Alternatively, grill (broil) beneath a very hot grill (broiler) for 5–8 minutes; reduce heat to medium; grill (broil) for a further 5 minutes or until meltingly tender.

5 Serve with the pistachios scattered over all.

SERVES 4

8 ripe medium-sized tomatoes, halved crosswise
3 pinches saffron stigmas
3 teaspoons caster sugar
1/2 teaspoon seasalt crystals
1/2 cinnamon stick or 5cm (2 in) piece of cassia, broken into fragments
2 tablespoons extra-virgin olive oil
2 teaspoons orange flower water
2 tablespoons blanched, skinned, slivered pistachios, to garnish

white cheese paste with olives and preserved lemons

In the souks, dairy products are on display in splendid rows. Goat's and sheep's milk cheeses are white, dense, salty and opinionated in flavour: the type suited to this recipe. I tasted this first as a filling inside a *briouat*, a triangular, crisp pastry. It is, however excellent as a snack in its own right.

SERVES 4–6

450g (1lb) salty, dry white cheese such as feta, goat's milk or sheep's milk cheese, crumbled
4 garlic cloves, crushed
75g ($^1/_3$–scant $^1/_2$ cup) thick, natural yoghurt
$^1/_2$ lemon, squeezed
seasalt flakes and black pepper, to taste
$^1/_2$ teaspoon dried oregano, za'atar or wild mint
3 preserved lemons (inner flesh discarded) each in 12 segments (see page 43)
100g ($^3/_4$ cup) salt-cured black olives
2 cos lettuces or 4 little gem lettuces

1 Mix the cheese, garlic, yoghurt, lemon juice and seasoning in a bowl using a fork (or hand-held electric beater) to a slightly lumpy paste.

2 Spoon into the centre of a decorative serving bowl or dish. Scatter the shreds and oregano, za'atar or wild mint on top.

3 Arrange a mound of preserved lemon bits at one side then a mound of olives opposite them. Overlap lettuce leaves between the two.

4 Serve as an appetizer for dipping into: take a scoop of cheese, an olive and a lemon piece rolled up inside each leaf wrapper. Eat in one bite.

byessar: broad (fava) bean purée

Moroccans get a look of longing in their eyes when this dish is discussed: it is a favourite comfort food and, protein-rich, a useful dietary basic too especially when some *khubz* bread triangles are dipped into it. A generous swirl of olive oil puts the finishing touch.

SERVES 4

250g (9oz) dried, skinned, split broad
   (fava) beans (*ful bissara*)
4 garlic cloves, chopped
1 teaspoon cumin seeds
1–1½ teaspoons seasalt flakes
5–6 tablespoons extra-virgin olive oil
½ teaspoon fresh or dried thyme, marjoram
   or oregano

TO SERVE
additional extra-virgin olive oil, to finish and warmed
   flatbreads of choice

1 Soak the beans in boiling water to cover them by at least 15cm (6 in) for 2 hours (or overnight if time allows).

2 Drain the beans. Cover with 900ml (4 cups) fresh water. Add the garlic and cumin. Bring to boiling; reduce to simmering, part-cover and cook for 1½ hours or until easy to crush. Use a pestle and mortar, a food processor or a vegetable mill (mouli) to purée the beans to a rough paste: do not overprocess. Stir in the salt to your taste. Stir in the olive oil to create a softish purée.

3 Serve in a bowl with the herbs, destalked, sprinkled on top. Drizzle over some extra olive oil at serving time. Eat this dip with bread.

tomato and roasted capsicum salad

Long green capsicums are by far the preferred type in Morocco, but it is acceptable to add some sweet, fruity red capsicums to certain recipes. Long white radishes, seen everywhere in the markets, are often called turnips: a confusing distinction.

SERVES 4–6

3 red capsicums, halved lengthwise
2 long green capsicums, halved lengthwise
4 large ripe beefsteak tomatoes or 350g (12oz) cherry tomatoes
4 small hot red or green chillies, finely sliced
1 bunch pink radishes or 1 long white radish, green tops discarded, sliced
6 tablespoons garlicky vinaigrette
25g (1oz) salted anchovy fillets in olive oil (optional)

1 Preheat the grill (broiler) to very hot. Set the halved capsicums, skin sides up on a foil-lined rack and grill (broil) as closely as possible to the heat source for 8–10 minutes or until charred and tender. (Or charcoal-grill the capsicums, skin sides down, as above, until charred.)

2 Seal the grilled (broiled) capsicum halves in a paper or plastic bag and leave to steam for 15 minutes.

3 Slice the tomatoes crosswise into rounds and set on a platter. If using cherry tomatoes, halve crosswise. Scatter the chillies over and then the sliced radishes.

4 Discard the skins, seeds and stems of the grilled (broiled) capsicums. Slice the flesh into 2cm ($^3/_4$ in) strips. Criss-cross the two colours over the radishes. Drizzle vinaigrette over all. (If using anchovies, scissor-snip them lengthwise into halves. Arrange these on top.) Serve this salad cool or briefly chilled.

lettuce and purslane salad with orange

Pretty, floppy green purslane leaves are greens not often seen nor appreciated in this country but they are certainly loved by Moroccans. I tasted a salad like this in a charming Moroccan restaurant in London. A rare treat for me and a surprise.

SERVES 6

1 cos lettuce, separated into leaves (optional)
350g (about 4 cups) fresh purslane or, if none is available, corn salad
1 small courgette (zucchini), in tiny dice
2 tablespoons argan oil or toasted sesame oil
1 red onion, skinned and very finely sliced
2 navel oranges or 3 blood oranges

SEASONING MIX
2 teaspoons hot paprika
1 teaspoon ground cassia or cinnamon
2 teaspoons caster sugar
$^1/_2$ teaspoon seasalt crystals

TO FINISH
2 teaspoons orange flower water or rose water

1 Cover a large serving dish with small whole cos leaves or halved large leaves if using. Toss on the purslane sprigs and courgette (zucchini) dice, and drizzle all over with the oil. Scatter the onion over the greens.

2 Remove the zest and pith from the oranges using a sharp, serrated stainless steel knife and discard. Slice the fruits into chunky double segments and set on top.

3 Use a pestle and mortar or electric spice grinder to reduce the paprika, cassia or cinnamon, sugar and seasalt to a rosy powder. Sprinkle this over the salad; add the scented water and serve the salad cool.

Illustrated on contents page.

cuajada herb-potato omelette

All around the Mediterranean, eggs are used to create delicious, substantial snacks, whether eaten for breakfast or as an appetizer or along with some soup as a late, quick, supper dish. Sometimes fresh peas are added; fragments of dried chilli, tomato dice or broad (fava) beans might be other possible additions.

1 Steam the potatoes for 20 minutes over boiling water using the top steamer section of a couscoussier or traditional steamer until soft. Alternatively boil them, unpierced and whole, in boiling salted water for 20 minutes, then drain, cool slightly and peel off and discard the skins.

2 Cube half the potatoes, and mash the remainder adding the cumin-seasoned salt, pepper, turmeric and half of the fresh coriander (cilantro). Stir in the potatoes.

3 Beat the eggs with a fork and stir into the potatoes. Preheat the oven to 200°C (400°F).

4 Set the base of a deep earthenware tagine, flameproof casserole or cast-iron frying pan over moderate heat. Pour in olive oil to a depth of nearly 1cm ($^1/_2$ in). Once it is very hot, pour in the egg mixture, spreading it using a fork.

5 Cook the omelette over direct heat for 5–8 minutes tipping the pan and letting the uncooked mixture trickle under the edges. Then transfer to the oven.

6 Bake for 15–18 minutes, until set, golden and puffy, piercing the omelette to let the oil soak into it. Scatter the remaining coriander (cilantro) over. Serve in scoops, squares or wedges, and pour off the excess oil (it is delicious, and useful in other recipes).

NOTE

This recipe could also make 4 or 5 individual omelettes; these take just 4 minutes cooking time initially; then 3 or 4 minutes extra in the oven.

SERVES 4 OR 5

650g (1lb 7oz) red-skinned, floury potatoes, halved lengthwise
1 teaspoon cumin-seasoned salt (see page 31)
1 teaspoon freshly ground black pepper
$^1/_4$ teaspoon ground turmeric
large handful coriander (cilantro) leaves, freshly chopped
8 large eggs
extra-virgin olive oil, for cooking

briouats with eggs and capers

If you are quick fingered and lucky, you may manage to cook these treats until the outside is crisp, the inside runny and yellow: it takes a little skill. (Cowards may soft boil the quails' eggs then shell them and use them in the filling.) *Briouats* delight in their very many forms, they can be tiny or large; rectangular or triangular; savoury or sweet; or even honey dipped. Small pies like these are called *briks* in Tunisia and Algeria and in Morocco's Rif Mountains. Since *ouarka* is round, half-circular pieces create triangle shapes best; filo rectangles create squares easily, but please yourself.

SERVES 4–5 (MAKES 18)

75g (3oz) preserved lemons (see page 43)
50g (1 cup) coarsely chopped fresh parsley, coriander (cilantro) or celery leaves
50g (1/3 cup) salted capers
1/4 teaspoon cumin-seasoned salt (see page 31)
9 ouarka sheets (*feuilles de brick)* or 275g (10oz) filo pastry (18 sheets)
75–100g (1/3–1/2 cup) ghee or clarified butter, melted, lukewarm, for brushing
18 quails' eggs
1 egg white, beaten with a fork
virgin olive oil, for deep frying

1 First make the filling. Discard the central flesh of the preserved lemons; slice their skins. Mix the lemon skins, herbs, capers and cumin-seasoned salt together. If using filo pastry, preheat the oven to 180°C (350°F).

2 Put one pastry sheet in front of you, keeping the remainder covered by a cloth or sheet of heavy plastic while you work.

3 If using ouarka sheets, slice a round sheet into half to give 2 semicircles. Brush one side generously with ghee. Set half a tablespoon of filling onto the corner of one semicircle on the unbuttered side. Fold over the point to enclose it. Fold again, then break one quail's egg in and continue to roll and fold, working quickly, until the pastry is used up and egg is neatly trapped inside, brushing the final joins with egg white. Continue the process until 9 are made.

4 If using ouarka sheets, deep-fry in batches of 2 in 10cm (4 in) of virgin olive oil heated to 180°C (350°F). Cook until crisp, about 3–4 minutes, turning halfway through. Continue with the remaining pastries until the first batch is cooked and ready. Repeat to make the next 9 *briouats*.

5 If using filo pastry rectangles, brush one side with ghee. Set a share of filling on the unbrushed side, at centre-base. Fold up the base flap then side flaps over it to cover it. Add the quail eggs. Continue to fold up and over to form a neat square, using egg white to seal final flaps. Brush finished *briouats* all over again with more ghee. Set them on a ghee-brushed oven tray. Bake the *briouats* for 20–25 minutes, turning them over halfway through. Cook until golden and crispy.

6 Eat while hot using your fingers.

harira (ramadan soup)

Harira soup is the soup most beloved of all Moroccans, with its ritual significance of being the food with which the fast days of Ramadan are joyfully broken. Oddly, it is traditionally served with sticky, honeyed pastries alongside in little saucers or some dates or other dried fruits. I have tasted this soup with rice and without; with bones always; with coriander (cilantro) inevitably. It is a truly wonderful soup. The last taste was in the famous *Place de Jemaa el F'na*, Marrakesh, on a cold spring evening. Bliss.

SERVES 6 (MAKES 3.5–4 LITRES)

2 large onions, sliced

50g (1 cup) flatleaf parsley, coarsely chopped

2 celery sticks, with leaves, sliced

1 teaspoon freshly ground black pepper

5cm (2 in) piece cassia or 1 cinnamon stick, broken into long shards

1 teaspoon ground turmeric

25g (3 tablespoons) ghee, clarified butter or s'men

500g (1lb) shoulder lamb chops, halved

6 chicken wings, halved (about 375g/13oz)

100g (3$^{1}/_{2}$oz) chicken hearts, necks or giblets (optional)

100g ($^{1}/_{2}$ cup) dried red lentils

50g (1 cup) fresh coriander (cilantro) leaves

1–1$^{1}/_{2}$ teaspoons salt, to taste

750ml (27fl oz) tomato passata (purée) or canned plum tomatoes, juiced in juicer or food-processed to a liquid

50g (8 tablespoons) fideuá (fine soup noodles or broken vermicelli)

2 pinches saffron stigma and 1 teaspoon seasalt crystals

TO SERVE
fresh coriander (cilantro) leaves; fresh lemon halves

1 Using a large, flameproof casserole, sauté the onions, parsley, celery, pepper, cassia and turmeric in the ghee for 5 minutes.

2 Add the lamb, chicken wings and chicken hearts. Continue sautéing for 20 minutes. Wash and drain the lentils then pound the coriander (cilantro) and salt briefly to a paste. Add these and the tomato to the pan. Cook hard for 15 minutes; pour in 1.5 litres (7 cups) of boiling water. Cook, covered, until the lentils are soft, the meats tender. Add the pasta.

3 Grind the saffron with the seasalt crystals to a powder. Sprinkle this in with the pasta. Cook for 15 minutes longer.

4 To serve, stir in the extra coriander (cilantro). Serve in individual bowls with lemon halves for squeezing.

NOTE

If you like, serve pitted dates stuffed with pistachio marzipan and pistachio shreds as an accompaniment.

fish

baby red mullet with green grapes and parsley

Using green grapes and a little chilli to stuff these pretty, delicate tasting fish seems to me a charming idea. The intense taste of the sea-fresh fish is complemented by these elements; the herbs and spices add even more finesse.

SERVES 4

12 baby red mullet, scaled, gutted
   (about 650–750g/1lb 7oz–1lb 10oz)
24 seedless green grapes, quartered
2 hot green and/or red chillies, finely chopped
25g ($^{1}/_{2}$ cup) flatleaf parsley, scissor-chopped
$^{1}/_{4}$ teaspoon grated nutmeg or allspice
24 wooden cocktail sticks (toothpicks),
   pre-soaked
2 tablespoons extra-virgin olive oil
seasalt crystals, to serve

1 Pat dry the red mullet, inside and out, using kitchen paper. Mix together the grapes, chillies, parsley and nutmeg. Push some of this inside each fish. Secure each using 2 pre-soaked wooden cocktail sticks (toothpicks).

2 Heat a non-stick pan until very hot. Pour in 1 tablespoon of the oil. Sizzle half the fish for 2 minutes on the first side, turn over and cook for 2 minutes on the second. Remove from the pan. Keep hot. Continue to cook the remaining fish the same way, using the second measure of oil.

3 If preferred, bake the prepared fish in one layer in a large, shallow, earthenware casserole that has been generously oiled. Drizzle the remaining oil over the fish. Cook at 230ºC (450ºF) for 10–12 minutes or until tender, fragrant and hot right through.

4 Serve the fish hot, salted lightly, with an olive- and orange-based salad, a baby leaf salad or some cracked wheat in vinaigrette.

chargrilled baby sardines with sweet stuffing

Around the ports and fishing villages of Morocco — and even inland — it is not surprising to see sardines stuffed with dried figs, dates, preserved lemons or bits of sugar-preserved fruits or even honey dates: little fruits sold in spice stalls which are a favourite nibble. Fish is often expensive inland, but sardines are affordable so tend to have many different treatments. This version is unusual and delicious.

SERVES 4 OR 6

8–12 small fresh sardines (about 500g/
   1lb 2oz), scales removed, gutted
seasalt flakes and ground pepper, to season
50g (3 tablespoons) pinenuts
25g (2 tablespoons) golden raisins (jumbo
raisins)
165g fresh or dried dates, pits discarded
   (1 cups pitted)
2 tablespoons fresh orange juice
1 teaspoon freshly shredded orange zest
2 tablespoons chopped fresh mint
wetted string or palm leaf strips, to tie
2 tablespoons extra-virgin olive oil

1 Use kitchen paper to wipe clean and dry the gut cavities of the sardines. Sprinkle inside with salt and pepper.

2 Use a sharp knife on a chopping board to chop and mix together the pinenuts, raisins, dates, juice and zest. Stir in the mint. Push some stuffing inside each fish. Secure each using a 25cm (10 in) long piece of wetted string or palm leaf strips. Knot each neatly.

3 Get the charcoal to a steady glow. Charcoal grill the sardines for 3 minutes on the first side. Turn, using tongs; charcoal grill for 2 minutes on the second side, or until tender but cooked right through.

4 Serve 2 or 3 sardines per person drizzled with some olive oil; unwrap and remove ties and eat using your fingers.

hut makalli with chermoula

I hunted in vain to find this well-known dish on any market stall in the famous *Place de Jemaa el F'na*, a magnificent square that must truly comprise the biggest, boldest, most extraordinary outdoor restaurant in the world. It has jugglers, snake charmers, water-sellers, medicine men hawking instant 'cures' and row after row of stalls doing a furious trade in aphrodisiac potions (for men only) as well as soups, nutty snacks, pickles, fondants, dried fruits, cookies, beignets and grills from goat's head to liver brochettes. Finally I found some *hut makalli* in a tiny back alley. Delicious, and homely too.

1 Remove and discard any bones from the fillets.

2 Make the coating mix. Put the seasalt, allspice berries, chilli, ginger and anise seeds into a mortar. Pound, using a pestle, to a gritty seasoning. Mix this into the cornmeal. Pour this into a large plate.

3 Heat the oil in a heavy deep fryer with a frying basket until it reaches 180ºC (350ºF).

4 Pour the milk into a saucer or plate. Dip four fillets first into the milk then into the coating mix. Press an even layer onto both sides. Deep fry for 3–4 minutes or until crusty, golden and aromatic. Remove. Keep hot. Repeat this process with the remaining prepared fillets.

5 Serve the hot fish in a twist of paper with some chermoula paste as seasoning, at the side, or in some flatbreads or *khubz* 'pockets'.

chermoula paste

Combine, in a mortar, 4 chopped garlic cloves, 1 teaspoon seasalt, 2 teaspoons hot paprika, 1/4 teaspoon cayenne pepper, 1/2 teaspoon black or white peppercorns, 1 teaspoon each of coriander and cumin seeds. Pound these hard to create a gritty powder. Squeeze in juice of 1/2 lemon and add enough extra-virgin olive oil to make a paste. Stir, use as a condiment, a sauce or a dip.

SERVES 4

8 freshwater or sea fish fillets or fillet pieces, each about 70g (2 1/2oz), (total 550g/ 1lb 4oz)

COATING MIX
1 tablespoon seasalt crystals
1 tablespoon allspice berries
1/2 teaspoon dried hot chilli flakes
1 tablespoon ground ginger
1 teaspoon anise seeds
100g (1 cup) medium cornmeal

virgin olive oil, for deep frying
90–120ml (6–8 tablespoons) milk or almond milk
chermoula paste, for seasoning (see left)
flatbreads or pocketed *khubz* (optional)

daurade with preserved lemons

Daurade, dorado or gilt-head bream: these are all names for the same, splendidly handsome and succulent sea fish. With very little effort such a fish can become the mainstay of a meal. Cumin is, with preserved lemon and a hint of the more acerbic lime, the perfect flavouring. Courgettes (zucchini) add a silky texture contrast at serving time.

SERVES 4

1 large daurade (gilt-head golden or pink bream), about 800g (1lb 12oz), scaled, gutted
4 tablespoons extra-virgin olive oil or sunflower oil
1 small fresh lime, in tiny dice (flesh, pith, zest)
1 tablespoon cumin-seasoned salt (see below)
3 preserved lemons, drained (see page 43)
5cm (2 in) chunk fresh ginger, skinned, in long shreds
2 medium courgettes (zucchini)
¼ teaspoon chilli flakes or cayenne

1 Slash the fish diagonally three times on each side. Set the bream in a large heatproof casserole or earthenware tagine, lightly brushed with a little of the oil.

2 Scatter over the tiny lime pieces; rub the cumin-seasoned salt into the slashes and into the gut cavity.

3 Scrape out the inner flesh of the preserved lemons. Keep it aside. Slice skins lengthwise into strips. Scatter half of these around the fish; add the ginger shreds. Drizzle half the remaining oil all over the fish.

4 Bake in an oven preheated to 200°C (400°F) for 30 minutes or until tender and aromatic.

5 Using a floating blade peeler or vegetable parer, cut the courgettes (zucchini) into long silky ribbons. Use these to cover a serving dish. Scatter the remaining lemon strips over.

6 Mix together the remaining oil, the chilli or cayenne and the reserved lemon fleshy pulp. Serve the fish and its garnishes on its bed of courgette (zucchini) salad, drizzled generously with the spiced aromatised oil. Serve hot, warm or cool.

cumin-seasoned salt

In a mortar, grind equal quantities of cumin seeds and seasalt crystals. This is the usual Moroccan seasoning mix.

boulettes de maquereau, sauce de tomates

Fish balls made from sardines or herring are a classic Moroccan dish and one that is also popular all around the Mediterranean. This variation using mackerel has a surprising finesse, but it is the mellow, sweet-salt-spicy tomato sauce that completes the pleasure.

SERVES 4 (MAKES 20–24)

BOULETTES

2 large fresh mackerel, filleted, about 800g
   (1lb 12oz) prepared weight
1 teaspoon seasalt flakes
2 tablespoons chermoula paste (see page 28)
4 tablespoons chopped celery leaves
50g (2oz) slice stale bread, crumbled
6 tablespoons flour, for coating
virgin olive oil or sunflower oil, for frying
celery leaves, to garnish (optional)

SAUCE DE TOMATES

450g (1lb) ripe tomatoes, finely diced
1 red onion, finely chopped
1 teaspoon cumin-seasoned salt (see page 31)
1 teaspoon paprika or hot paprika
1 tablespoon white sugar
3 tablespoons extra-virgin olive oil

1 Make the sauce: combine the ingredients in a heavy-based saucepan. Cook, stirring and mashing, over high heat for 10 minutes, uncovered, adding 3–4 tablespoons of water to create a rich, reduced and thick sauce. Rub through a strainer, if you like, to remove the skin.

2 Remove or slice away as much skin and as many bones as possible from the mackerel and discard. Cut the fish into 1cm (½ in) pieces. Put the fish, the salt, chermoula paste, celery leaves and breadcrumbs into a food processor or large, heavy mortar. Blitz or pound to a paste. Do not overprocess.

3 Form walnut-sized portions into neat balls, squeezing and compacting them. Roll them in some flour, to coat evenly.

4 Heat 1cm (½ in) depth of oil in a large tagine or a heavy-based frying pan until it reaches 180°C (350°F). Fry the boulettes for 4–5 minutes, rolling them gently around in the pan to brown them evenly.

5 Serve them hot in a pool of the hot fragrant sauce, garnished with celery leaves if you like.

king prawn (jumbo shrimp) brochettes

Whenever I travel I always buy some brochettes or metal skewers. Workmanlike and handsome, these remind me of far-off meals in wonderful places long after I have returned home, such as this recipe which is luxuriously simple but superb.

SERVES 4

12 large, raw king prawns (jumbo shrimp) in
   the shell (about 500g/1lb 2oz)
6 garlic cloves, crushed
50g (1 cup) chopped fresh parsley
50g (1 cup) chopped fresh coriander (cilantro)
40g (⅓ cup) blanched almonds, sliced
3 tablespoons extra-virgin olive oil
4 metal skewers
fresh limes, sliced, to squeeze (optional)

Illustrated on title page.

1 Make long slashes down the back of each prawn (shrimp). Remove and discard the long black vein (intestinal tract) from each one.

2 Combine the crushed garlic, parsley, coriander (cilantro), almonds and 1 tablespoonful of the oil in a mortar. Pound using a pestle to make a rough herb stuffing. Push a share of the stuffing into each slashed king prawn (jumbo shrimp). Loop in rows of 3 onto each skewer.

3 Preheat a griddle or large non-stick frying pan. Griddle-cook the prawns for 2 minutes on one side; turn and cook for 1 minute on the second side, or until the flesh is pearly white and the shells turn rosy and smell aromatic. Turn off the heat. Leave to stand for a few minutes.

4 Serve, drizzled with the remaining oil, on folded flatbreads, rice, pasta ribbons or green leafy salad, with lime slices if you like.

meat

lamb tagine with quince, prunes and almonds

These splendid stews, cooked and served in their conical dishes, are a delight and have many seasonal and regional variations. I ate one similar to this in the Atlas foothills.

SERVES 4–6

4 garlic cloves, crushed
1kg (2lb 4oz) boneless leg of lamb, in 5cm
  (2 in) chunks
2 teaspoons mild paprika or paprika flakes
$\frac{1}{2}$ teaspoon cayenne pepper or dried chilli flakes
1 teaspoon ground ginger or allspice
1 teaspoon cumin-seasoned salt (see page 31)
1 tablespoon date or pomegranate molasses
1 large fresh quince, peeled, cored, cut into 12, or
  4 canned quince pieces, halved
8 prunes or other dried plums
8 honey dates (see page 10) (optional)
juice of 1 orange
2 carrots, cut in strips
4 tablespoons ghee, clarified butter or s'men
2 red onions, in segments
50g ($\frac{1}{3}$ cup) whole blanched almonds

1 Rub the garlic all over the lamb. In a large tagine or flameproof casserole, mix the spices and cumin-seasoned salt and toss the meat cubes in this. To 250ml (1 cup plus 2 tablespoons) boiling water add the molasses and stir. Add to the tagine. If using fresh quince, add it at this stage.

2 Bring the pan contents to boiling. Cover and reduce the heat to simmering. Cook for 1½ hours undisturbed.

3 Uncover the pot. Set the canned, drained quince pieces, if using, decoratively around the edge with the prunes and honey dates, pushing them down into the liquid. Pour over the orange juice and another 200ml (scant 1 cup) boiling water and add the carrot strips. Cover the pan; continue to cook for a further 30 minutes.

4 Ten minutes before serving time, heat the ghee and sauté the onions in a frying pan until browned and collapsed. Remove them to the centre of the tagine. Brown the almonds in the same pan; scatter over the tagine and serve hot.

buried meat couscous

What a fabulous surprise: a cone of hot, fragrant grain covering nuggets of tender, fruit-enhanced, olive-seasoned beef. Serve beef this way and intrigue your guests.

SERVES 4–6

300g (2 cups) 'instant' couscous, medium (moyen) type
4 tablespoons extra-virgin olive oil and 2 extra for
  kneading couscous
1kg (2lb 4oz) lean stewing beef, e.g. topside in 4cm
  (1½ in) pieces
20 tiny white onions, peeled, each studded with a clove
2 bunches fresh or dried bay leaves
2 tablespoons pomegranate molasses
200ml (scant 1 cup) pomegranate juice
4 preserved lemons (see page 43)
100g ($\frac{2}{3}$ cup) salt-cured black olives
1 teaspoon roughly cracked black peppercorns
6 fresh apricots, halved, stoned
salt, chopped parsley and ghee, to season couscous
1 teaspoon paprika, to garnish

1 Wash and drain the couscous then knead it with your fingers to break up lumps; leave to stand. Sprinkle with 1 tablesoon of oil and rub in evenly with your fingers. Repeat this process again.

2 Heat the olive oil in a large couscoussier base. Add half the beef and onions, and brown well for 5 minutes. Remove and brown the remaining beef. Add the bay leaves, molasses, juice, and 100ml (scant ½ cup) boiling water. Add the lemons, olives and peppercorns.

3 Bring the pan contents to boiling; cover, reduce to simmering and cook for 1¼ hours or until tender. Add the apricots. Cover again; cook for a further 15 minutes.

4 Fit the steamer to the top of the couscoussier base and line it with wetted muslin. Add the prepared couscous and set this over the beef; cover tightly. Cook for 20 minutes or until the couscous is plump and fluffy. Lift out the couscous in its muslin and transfer to a bowl; mix in some salt, parsley and ghee, tossing with two forks. Pour the stew into a dish and pile the couscous in a cone on top, sprinkled with paprika.

berber mechoui

Some months ago I sat in a grandiloquent velvet, silk and wool tent in a massive kasbah complex, just outside Marrakesh eating mechoui: a crisp, tender forequarter of lamb, in the company of a handsome Berber companion. The food came in a domed metal dish, fragrant on its bed of fresh mint. To season it we had bowls of salt and of cumin. It was the second course of an amazing feast.

A whole, young lamb, cooked slowly over charcoal, on a revolving spit, out of doors, or cooked in a domed outdoor oven, is a festive dish, famed throughout Morocco. Because this process takes hours of slow, patient turning and basting and attention, the practical home equivalent could be a large forequarter or leg, cooked slowly in the oven, for 12 hours, undisturbed, at very low heat until it falls into tender shreds at your touch. Pull off and savour the hot, crispy meat using fingers: revel in the earthiness and allure of this magnificent dish.

SERVES 8–12

4.75kg (10lb 8oz) forequarter or 3kg (6lb 8oz) leg
   mountain, rare-breed or pre-salé lamb, shank intact
12 garlic cloves, halved lengthwise
24 sprigs flatleaf parsley
24 x 1cm (1/2 in) cubes of cold butter, ghee or lamb fat
fresh mint bunches, to garnish
seasalt flakes and freshly ground cumin seeds,
   to serve

1 Make incisions evenly all over the fleshier sections of the meat, then push in a garlic piece, a little bit of parsley and a cube of fat inside each cut.

2 Set the roast in a large shallow roasting pan or on a baking sheet. Turn to oven to 110°C (225°F), set the lamb in the oven and cook, utterly undisturbed, for 12 hours.

3 Serve the meat on a fresh mint-lined metal platter or tray. Have the seasonings alongside. Encourage guests to eat using clean fingers and have scented water and napkins available, also copious wine, water and/or juice to drink.

chicken kdra with saffron, chickpeas and rice

Recently I had the brief joy of being a student at *La Maison Arabe*'s cooking school in its glamorous country estate outside Marrakesh, where a small but dedicated team teach novices to cook traditional Moroccan recipes. The term *kdra* refers to pale blanquette-like stews, gently cooked, often with lots of tender onions sweetening the mix. This one contains canned chickpeas and is enlivened with lemon juice and saffron. Unusually it also has rice, which gently thickens the sauce. This is the kind of stew above which couscous is traditionally steamed.

SERVES 6

400g (14oz) can chickpeas (drained weight
   240g/8¹/₂ oz)
1 preserved lemon (see page 43)
4 pinches saffron stigma, briefly pan-toasted
1 teaspoon seasalt crystals
1.5kg (3lb 4oz) chicken joints
1 teaspoon ground ginger
¹/₂ teaspoon ground turmeric
2 tablespoons clarified butter, ghee or s'men
2 handfuls fresh flatleaf parsley and coriander
   (cilantro), chopped, mixed
2 Spanish onions, halved, sliced
25g (1 oz) long-grained white rice, washed, drained
2 lemons, halved

1 Pour some boiling water over the chickpeas in a sieve; loosen, remove and discard as many skins as possible. Scrape out the pulpy flesh from the preserved lemon. Reserve both parts.

2 Grind the saffron with the salt to a powder, using a pestle and mortar. Rub half of this over the chicken with all of the ginger, the turmeric, butter and herbs to coat it well.

3 Put the seasoned chicken, the onions and the preserved lemon pulp into a large tagine or flameproof casserole. Bring to sizzling; cover and cook for 10 minutes or until the chicken is part browned. Turn the joints over, add the preserved lemon skin and 350ml (1¹/₂ cups) water.

4 Add the chickpeas. Cover and bring back to simmering; cover again; cook for 20 minutes longer. Add the rice, stir, cover and simmer for 20 minutes more or until the rice is tender, sauce somewhat thickened and chickpeas hot. Squeeze the lemons over all.

5 Scatter the remaining saffron-salt over; cover; stand for 5 minutes then serve hot with couscous, torn breads or rice.

roasted chicken with olives, almonds and preserved lemons

A classic roast, made altogether new by the favourite Moroccan additions of s'men, olives, almonds and preserved lemons, which, in this recipe, keep their soft fleshy interiors intact.

SERVES 4

1.75kg (3lb 12oz) farm-reared, ideally corn-fed, chicken
4 garlic cloves, crushed to a pulp
1 teaspoon seasalt flakes
3 tablespoons soft ghee, s'men or clarified butter
3 preserved lemons (see below, right)
1 handful fresh thyme and marjoram sprigs, plus extra
   to scatter
50g (2 oz) blanched almonds
200g (1¹/₂ cups) cracked green olives or dry-cured
   black olives or a mix

1 Preheat the oven to 200°C (400°F). Pat the chicken dry inside and out using kitchen paper. Rub some garlic and salt over the inner and outer surfaces then some ghee over all. Push 1 preserved lemon inside the body with a handful of fresh herb sprigs.

2 Set the bird, breast up in a pan. Scatter in the remaining herbs, the almonds and the other preserved lemons, each separated into 'petals', halved. Push these in, under and around the edges of the bird. Pour in about 60ml (¹/₄ cup) of water. Roast uncovered for 30 minutes.

3 Turn the bird onto one breast. Set the olives around it and continue to cook at the temperature of 180°C (350°F) for a further 25 minutes; turn bird onto its other breast, cook for a final 25 minutes. Test the bird for doneness: juices from its thigh should run clear when pierced.

4 Turn the chicken breast up. Add 4 tablespoons of boiling water to the pan and stir to mix. Turn off the oven leaving the door slightly ajar. Leave the bird to stand for 10 minutes. Carve the chicken and serve, adding some of the caramelised lemon bits and sticky pan juice.

preserved lemons

Sterilize a 750ml (27fl oz) glass jar with a lid. Have 10 lemons, scrubbed, dried, and 125g (4¹/₂oz) coarse rock salt, seasalt crystals or kosher salt. Cut 2 intersecting cuts almost to the base of 6 lemons. Push 2 tablespoons of salt into each. Sprinkle 8 tablespoons of salt into the jar. Wedge 3 salted lemons into it, cut sides up. Push in 9 peppercorns. Repeat with the other 3 cut lemons, and 9 more peppercorns. Add the juice from the remaining 4 lemons. Dissolve any remaining salt in 50ml (¹/₄ cup) boiled water then cool. Top up the jar so that the lemons are covered. Fasten the sterilized lids tightly. Leave in a cool, dark place for 4 weeks, inverting the jar once a week. Remove each lemon using a sterilized utensil. Reseal and store again.

rabbit stuffed with pinenuts and perfumed orange

Moroccan cooks enjoy game and it is an education to visit a country market and see live birds and small game animals in cages about to be butchered on demand. There is a remarkable lack of fuss or of smell: the prepared creatures look pristine, often with perfect, unblemished skins. Rabbits, already shot and hung in geometric ranks, may well turn into an elaborate dish such as this one. Nuts, not breadcrumbs, make the stuffing sumptuously delicious, and argan oil adds unusual pleasure.

SERVES 4

1 prepared wild or cultivated rabbit, heart and liver
   intact
seasalt crystals and black peppercorns, ground using
   pestle and mortar, to taste
2 tablespoons argan or extra-virgin olive oil
400g (1¾ cups) pinenuts, chopped
100g (scant 1 cup) chopped hazelnuts or walnuts
shredded zest and juice of 1 flavourful orange
   (bergamot type, if available)
100g (2 cups) fresh parsley and celery leaves, mixed,
   finely chopped
1 tablespoon orange flower water
juice of 1 lemon, freshly squeezed
2–3 tablespoons honey
500g (1lb 2oz) fine green beans, trimmed
salt, to season

1 Pat dry the rabbit. Cut it crosswise into four: a front section, saddle section and two legs. Season using salt and pepper all over. Heat the oil in a large flameproof casserole and brown the rabbit lightly on both sides, in two batches, for about 2 minutes each batch.

2 Using a pestle and mortar or food processor pound or blitz together in bursts, the nuts, zest, herbs and orange flower water to a rough paste. Sprinkle in enough orange and lemon juice and honey to help it create a sticky rough paste, pounding again to amalgamate it.

3 Remove the rabbit joints from the pan. Push an equal share of the stuffing up and under each portion so it clings neatly to the hollows.

4 Arrange half of the beans in the base of the same pan. Add the rabbit pieces, stuffing sides downwards. Pour over enough water to nearly cover, adding any remaining orange and lemon juices. Add a generous measure of salt.

5 Bring the pan contents to simmering; cover tightly, cook for 40–45 minutes or until the rabbit is fragrant and tender and the stuffing has thickened the pan liquids. Boil the remaining green beans separately for 3–4 minutes, drain and add. Allow 1 rabbit joint and its stuffing per diner, along with a share of sauce and the beans. Eat hot or warm.

pigeons, kefta-stuffed, with baby vegetables

Pigeons are one of the pleasures of the Moroccan table. Plump squabs, tender but fleshy, are often used in *b'stilla*, but this treatment, filling them with a rich meat and grain stuffing, is particularly indulgent: succulent, suitable for a feast, anniversary or celebration. Enjoy this dish with a robust red wine. Poussins or partridges could be used instead of pigeons.

SERVES 4

2 squabs (young, tender pigeons), halved lengthwise
4 garlic cloves, crushed
2 tablespoons s'men, ghee or virgin olive oil
200ml (scant 1 cup) grape juice
300ml (1¼ cups) chicken stock
600g (1lb 4oz) assorted young tender vegetables:
    podded peas, sugar snap peas, small quartered
    turnips, skinned broad (fava) beans etc.
fresh coriander (cilantro) leaves, to garnish

KEFTA

40g (⅓ cup) cracked wheat or cracked barley
350g (12oz) minced (ground) chicken or beef
2 teaspoons cumin-seasoned salt (see page 31)
½ teaspoon black peppercorns, coarsely crushed
2 teaspoons *ras el hanout* (see right)
8 tablespoons chopped fresh coriander (cilantro)
1 onion, coarsely grated
2 tablespoon grated beef fat or suet

1 Rub the halved pigeons, inside and out, with the garlic.

2 Make the kefta: pour 100ml (scant ½ cup) of boiling water over the cracked wheat. Leave for 10 minutes then strain off all liquid using a sieve. Pound or mix together the soaked grain, minced meat, cumin-seasoned salt, pepper, spice mix and fresh coriander (cilantro) with the grated onion and beef fat to create a dense meat paste.

3 Mound a portion of kefta under each pigeon half, rounding so it covers the bone ends and stays neatly in place.

4 Heat the s'men or ghee in a flameproof casserole or frying pan and brown the pigeons, skin sides down for 5 minutes. Turn them using tongs and sauté the stuffing side for 3 minutes.

5 Pour in the juice and stock. Bring the liquid back to the boil, reduce the heat, cover and simmer the stew for 30 minutes.

6 Add the baby vegetables. Part-cover the pan. Cook for 5–10 minutes more depending on the size and age of the vegetables. Stir and serve hot with fresh coriander (cilantro) sprigs as garnish.

ras el hanout

This famous, complex Moroccan spice mix translates as 'top of the shop' which defines it importance as seasoning and health 'tonic'. Hundreds of recipes exist: it's best to make your own.

Combine and dry-toast in a frying pan until fragrant 2 tablespoons each of cumin and coriander seeds, black peppercorns, sliced dried ginger root, and a cinnamon stick, broken. Add 20 cloves, 20 allspice berries, 10 dried rosebuds, 10 green cardamom pods, half a nutmeg, rated, and 2 tablespoons of salt. Pound, using a pestle and mortar or electric spice grinder, to a powder. Store in an airtight container. Use in game dishes, tagines, stews, some couscous and rice dishes.

quodban (beef shashliks)

In her superb book about Moroccan cuisine, author Paula Wolfert describes skewered, spicy shashliks she tasted near the town of Khemisett, Morocco. They were pushed into salty, crusty, barley-coated breads. Here is my interpretation of her interesting recipe, made using beef rather than the more usual lamb and a variety of different seasonings. Shashliks like this were being cooked on charcoal burners at wayside cafés in the foothill villages of the Atlas mountains near Imlil, on the day we visited.

SERVES 4

800g (1lb 12oz) boneless beef rump or sirloin,
   in 2.5cm (1 in) cubes
300g (10oz) beef fat, in thin squares (not cubes) about
   5mm (1/4 in) thick
4 tablespoons chopped fresh parsley
4 tablespoons chopped fresh coriander (cilantro) leaves
   and extra coriander (cilantro) sprigs, to serve
cumin-seasoned salt (see page 31), to taste
black pepper, freshly pounded or ground, to taste
1 tablespoon coriander seeds, freshly pounded or
   ground, to taste
4 flatbreads, ideally coated with cracked barley grains
   (see page 54) or other flatbreads of choice
3 red onions
8 metal skewers
2 tablespoons pomegranate molasses (optional)

1 Mix all the ingredients, beef, fat, herbs, cumin-seasoned salt, pepper and coriander, together in a non-reactive container. Leave to dry-marinate overnight in the refrigerator, well covered.

2 Make the barley-coated flatbreads (see recipe page 54).

3 Preheat the grill (broiler) or charcoal barbecue to a medium heat. Segment the onions into 'petals' cut one by one from halved red onions, each layer separated out.

4 Push onto each metal skewer two pieces of meat, one slice of fat, several onion 'petals', then repeat this with the remaining skewers. Continue until all the ingredients have been used up.

5 Grill (broil) or barbecue the shashliks about 4–5cm (1½–2 in) from the heat source, turning each one over after 4–5 minutes. Proceed to cook the second sides. (In Morocco meat tends to be well cooked.)

6 Serve the meat, once removed from the skewers, folded inside the flatbreads. Glaze by brushing on some pomegranate molasses, if liked.

b'stilla with pigeon and eggs

B'stilla is one of the most magnificent achievements of the Moroccan kitchen. I am fortunate to have eaten this Moroccan pie made with chicken, with seafood, with pigeon and I am told that quail, pheasant and partridge are popular fillings. At a grand celebration for lots of people it is a superb first course: layers of softly curded egg; layers of nutty marzipan-like mixture; and the best, the bone-in poultry (but bone it if you prefer.) Do not let the long recipe deter you: this is a *pièce de resistance*.

SERVES 8–10

3 squabs (young, tender pigeons), total weight
   about 1.2kg (2lb 12oz), or 6 quail,
   3 partridge or 2 poussins, if none available
6 garlic cloves, crushed to a pulp
1 handful fresh flatleaf parsley and coriander
   (cilantro), mixed (about 30g/$\frac{1}{2}$ cup)
1 large onion, thinly sliced
4 pinches powdered saffron (optional)
2 teaspoons salt and 1 teaspoon freshly
   ground black pepper
2.5cm (1 in) fresh ginger, peeled, shredded
5cm (2 in) piece of cassia or 1$\frac{1}{2}$ cinnamon
   sticks, crushed into fragments
2 tablespoons extra-virgin olive oil
225g (1$\frac{1}{2}$ cups) whole blanched almonds
75g ($\frac{1}{2}$ cup) sieved icing (confectioners')
   sugar or more, as needed
2 tablespoons freshly squeezed lemon juice
6 large eggs, fork-whisked
250g (9oz) clarified butter, ghee, unsalted
   butter or s'men
400g (14oz) or 14 large filo pastry sheets or
   12 ouarka sheets (*feuilles de brick*)
1 tablespoon orange flower water
3 teaspoons ground cinnamon

1 Rub the pigeons all over with garlic. Push some of the herbs and onion slices inside each; sprinkle the saffron over. Put the birds, remaining herbs, onion and salt, pepper, ginger and cassia fragments with 750ml (3$\frac{1}{2}$ cups) hot water into a large flameproof casserole. Heat to boiling; cover and simmer for 1 hour.

2 Heat the oil and stir-fry the almonds over high heat until they become medium-dark. Cool, drain, reserving the oil, and chop or grind but leave gritty. Reserve half of the icing (confectioners') sugar and grind the cassia in a spice grinder with the remainder. Mix this with the almonds; keep aside.

3 Remove and drain the birds. Remove and keep all the meat; discard bones if you wish. Pour the stock through a sieve, discarding aromatics. Return it to the pan and fast-boil over high heat until the volume reduces to 400ml (1$\frac{3}{4}$ cups).

4 Whisk in the juice and the eggs over medium heat and continue cooking and whisking for about 3 minutes until they form scrambled curds. Remove from the heat, drain using a sieve, discarding the stock. Cool then keep aside.

5 Break or cut the pigeon into bite-sized pieces. Heat the clarified butter in a saucepan with the reserved oil. Pour a thin layer of butter-oil into a loose-based cake tin or baking dish about 22.5cm (9 in) in diameter. Keep the rest warm.

6 Preheat the oven to 220°C (450°F). Unwrap the pastry sheets or rounds and cover with a cloth. Overlap 4 sheets to cover the base of the tin with 4 layers, with the pastry overhanging the edge; brush well with butter-oil. Spread half of the almond mix over the pastry and sprinkle with orange flower water.

7 Take 4 more pastry sheets; fold them into halves. Set on a baking sheet, brush with butter-oil and bake them for 5 minutes or until crispy. Set 2 of these oven-crisped sheets over the nut layer, overlapped. Cover with the pigeon. Layer in the drained 'curds'. Top with the remaining almond-sugar mix.

8 Top with the last 2 crisp pastry sheets. Cover these with 4 more, overlapped, pastry sheets, buttered well. Roll and fold up the overlaps into a neat, curved roll just inside the rim: try to make a neat circle. Brush again with butter-oil.

9 Bake the *b'stilla* for 20 minutes at 230°C (450°F). Remove and tip out excess butter. Continue baking for 15–20 minutes at 200°C (400°F) or until crisp.

10 Serve the *b'stilla* as it is in its dish or unmould it. Present the pie, its top layer dusted with sieved icing (confectioners') sugar. Make neat parallel lines or criss-cross patterns of ground cinnamon on top using a knife edge as a guide.

breads and sweet things

moroccan khubz flatbreads

Standing just inside the walls of the Medina, my guide Khalina and I saw several small children with cloth-covered trays on their heads, walking towards an ancient door. This was the community bakery. In ageless tradition the locals prefer to let the expert use his huge oven to bake their breads rather than have to fuel and prepare their own ovens, even if they have them. The breads that we tasted, sometimes round, often oval, sometimes criss-cross patterned, were wonderful. A mixture of flours is most usual: cracked grains or aromatic seeds the toppings. Bread is and everyday necessity, an everyday delight.

SERVES 3 (MAKES 3 OVAL LOAVES)

500g (3¹/₂ cups) unbleached white flour or
   strong white bread flour
200g (1¹/₂ cups) wholewheat or strong
   wholemeal flour
2 teaspoons sugar
1¹/₂ teaspoons salt
2 x 7g (¹/₄oz) sachets, micronised, fast-
   acting yeast
220ml (scant 1 cup) lukewarm milk
3 teaspoons toasted sesame seeds
4 teaspoons anise or caraway seeds
medium cornmeal, for shaping
virgin olive oil or argan oil, for oiling

1 Sift the flours, sugar and salt into a large, shallow bowl. Stir in the yeast. Add the warm milk, mixed with 300ml (1¹/₄ cups) warm water, into a well in the dry ingredients. Stir well to mix. Shape it into a softish mound. Sprinkle in the seeds.

2 Knead hard, using your clenched knuckles (not your palm) pushing down then out for 8–10 minutes. If using a food mixer and dough hook, beat on low speed for 5 minutes.

3 Divide the dough into three equal pieces. Grasp one ball in your fist to create a cone shape. Rotate the wide end around inside the bowl's cornmeal-covered surface 5 or 6 times. Repeat with the next two.

4 Pat and stretch each piece of dough into an oval, dimpling it with your fingertips. Set on 2 oiled baking sheets.

5 Slide each baking sheet and its contents inside a large (oiled inside) heavy plastic bag. Seal. Leave to rise in a warm place for 1¹/₂–2 hours. If you like, use a knife point to run a border in 2cm (³/₄ in) from the edge then cut similar light, criss-cross patterns inside the border.

6 Bake in a fan (convection) oven at 200°C (400°F) for 10–15 minutes. Reduce the heat to 150°C (300°F) and cook for 20 minutes more or until golden, risen and hollow-sounding when tapped on the base. Eat warm, torn or cut into triangular pieces. (If making 6 half-sized breads, bake them for 10 minutes at 200°C (400°F) then 12–15 minutes at the lower temperature.)

VARIATION: FLATBREADS COATED WITH CRACKED BARLEY GRAINS

Use the basic bread recipe but substitute 100g (scant 1 cup) of the wholemeal flour with finely ground barley flour, from wholefood stores. Instead of shaping the dough into 3, shape it into 8, rolling it out thinly. Wet it; scatter over some rock salt and a few cracked barley grains. Bake the same way as the half-sized breads but reduce the time at the lower temperature by half.

marrakesh 'pizza' breads

Although we hunted high and low on a recent visit to Morocco, my guide and I never managed to find any market stall selling these outrageously rich, delicious spicy breads. This recipe is based on one from the book *Moroccan Cuisine* by Paula Wolfert, a wonderful source of food lore, traditions and authentic recipes.

SERVES 4 (MAKES 4 LARGE
OR 8 SMALL BREADS)

275g (2½ cups) unbleached white flour or
   strong white bread flour

7g (¼oz) sachet, micronised, fast-acting yeast

1 teaspoon salt

2 teaspoons clear honey

100g (½ cup) grated or diced lamb, mutton or
   beef suet

8 spring onions (scallions), finely chopped

1 teaspoon each of ground cumin, paprika,
   dried chilli fragments and salt

1 handful mixed flatleaf parsley and marjoram,
   chopped

2 tablespoons ghee, unsalted butter or s'men,
   melted

1 Sift together the flour, yeast and salt into a large bowl. Stir in about 200–225ml (scant 1 cup–1 cup) lukewarm water which has had the honey dissolved in it. Stir and mix to create a soft dough. Knead using the knuckles for about 8 minutes or until the dough feels elastic and looks smooth and silky.

2 Mix together the grated fat, spring onions (scallions), the three spices and salt, and the herbs. Have this mix ready to use as filling.

3 Divide the dough into 4 or 8 balls. Pat and stretch one out to a 20 x 30cm (8 x 12 in) rectangle. (For 8 breads make 10 x 15cm/4 x 6 in rectangles.)

4 Spread a portion of the filling over the centre quarter of the flattened dough. Fold the sides over it; then fold in the near flap then the far flap. Press down, to make a rectangle of enveloped dough. Use a rolling pin or your hands to press, stretch and flatten the stuffed dough to the size of the original rectangle.

5 Repeat the process to use all the dough pieces. Leave the finished rectangles of dough in a warm place to rise for 30 minutes.

6 Heat a large, flat, heavy griddle or large non-stick or cast-iron frying pan until very hot. Prick the first two 'pizzas' in 9 places, both sides, then slide into the hot pan. Cook for 8 minutes or so (about 4 minutes for small) on each side or until risen, browned, crusty and aromatic. Brush both sides with ghee or butter and remove from the pan.

7 Continue this process with the remaining 'pizzas'. They are kept rich, moist and flaky by the internal fat, which trickles out and bastes them from inside. Serve hot, brushed with more ghee.

NOTE

If a griddle is impractical or unavailable, fast-bake the 'pizzas' in an oven preheated to 220°C (425°F) for 15–20 minutes (12–15 minutes for small), turning them over half way.

gazelles' horns (kal el ghzal)

These plump, crescent-shaped pastries with fragrant, soft, orange-scented almond paste interiors should be delicate with fragile, easily broken pastry exteriors. The best of those I've tasted were sublime, but over-baking or heavy-handed pastry spoils them. Debates rage over the precise colour, the shape, its significance, the proper names and whether egg wash and a dusting of icing (confectioners') sugar can be called authentic or not. For me, the contrast between frangible pastry and gooey filling is a joy. Once tried these are never forgotten. My thanks to Ben and Omar who guided me through the intricacies.

MAKES 40

1kg (2lb 4oz) home-made almond paste (see page 61)
1 large egg, beaten with 1 tablespoon orange flower water
sieved icing (confectioners') sugar (optional)

PASTRY
275g (2½ cups) plain white flour, plus 75g (¾ cup) extra for mixing and rolling out
½ teaspoon salt
65g (5 tablespoons) s'men, ghee or clarified butter, melted
150ml (⅔ cup) orange flower water plus 2 tablespoons cool water

1 Divide the almond paste into 40 x 25g (1oz) balls. Roll each into a 10cm (4 in) sausage shape. Chill.

2 Make the pastry by sifting together the first measure of flour and the salt into a bowl. Make a well in the centre. Pour in the liquid s'men, flower water and cool water, mixed. Stir to a sticky dough, adding some of the extra flour to create a sticky dough, soft and pliable.

3 Knead in its bowl for 3 minutes. Rest for 5 minutes. Knead for 3 minutes more. Aim for a silky-smooth dough. Quarter it and dust one quarter with some flour. Roll it out thinly to about 50cm (20 in) in diameter. Cut it into 10 ovals each about 12cm (4½ in) length. Set an almond paste 'sausage' on each of the ovals. Brush the paste and dough with egg wash.

4 Fold in the end flaps, roll up and seal the pastry edges then curve both inwards, creating a gazelle horn or crescent shape. Position them, with the seams beneath. Pinch both ends to neat points. Once 10 are made transfer, using a palette knife, to a lightly oiled baking sheet. Make another 10 using a second pastry quarter. Transfer these as well. Repeat until all 40 are completed, setting these on oiled baking sheets.

5 Brush the pastries all over with remaining egg wash. Bake each batch in an oven preheated to 200°C (400°F) (180°C/350°F if using a fan/convection oven) for 12–16 minutes. Dust with icing (confectioners') sugar if you like. Serve warm or cool, or store airtight, once cold, for up to two weeks.

beghrir (honeycomb griddle cakes)

The elegant *Maison Arabe*, in Marrakesh, was where first I tasted these delightful bubbly pancakes. On the tray also came lovely Echiré butter; home-made preserves of orange and strawberry and superb, spice-enhanced, scalding hot coffee. Delicate yoghurt sat nearby and fresh orange juice. Since savouring this fascinating breakfast I've also learned that some Moroccans serve these pancakes alongside fried eggs garnished with fresh coriander (cilantro) and a few black olives: an idea worth trying. Since these batter-cakes cook on one side only, they are quick to cook, very easy, and respond to freezing and gentle reheating.

MAKES 24–28

200g (1 1/3 cups) plain, fine semolina (not semolina flour)
50g (1/2 cup) plain, white, wheat flour
1 x 7g (1/4oz) sachet, micronised, fast-acting yeast
1/2 teaspoon salt
1 large egg, whisked with 200ml (1 cup minus
  2 tablespoons) lukewarm water
1 tablespoon clear flower-scented honey
50g (4 tablespoons) s'men, ghee, clarified butter or
  salted butter

1 Sieve together the semolina, flour, yeast and salt into a bowl.

2 Whisk together the egg, lukewarm water and honey, and pour this all at once into the dry ingredients. Whisk for 1 minute; stand the batter, covered, in a warm place for 30 minutes or until visibly bubbly.

3 Preheat a non-stick electric griddle or heat a griddle pan or frying pan until fairly hot. Smear almost a teaspoonful of s'men over the hot surface. Using a 15ml (1 tablespoon) measure, ladle out pancakes onto the hot surface. Reduce heat to medium-low. Leave the batter-cakes to cook gently from underneath. After 3 to 3 1/2 minutes the wet, shiny top surface will have dulled to dry: well cooked through. They are ready at this point.

4 Remove using a palette knife; keep hot under a cloth. Continue to cook the remaining batter mixture in batches until all are completed. Serve them warm with whatever accompaniments you prefer.

NOTE

Adding some fresh lemon juice and rose water to natural yoghurt and some crushed green cardamom pods or cloves to your coffee can create the illusion that you are breakfasting in Morocco: a joy.

'snake' pastry (m'hencha)

To my joy, I was taught this famously delicious and unusual recipe while working with the renowned author–cook, Claudia Roden, on one of her prize-winning, illustrated food features for the *Observer Magazine* many years ago. Her instructions were poetic but precise: the results were splendid, grandiloquent. This recipe is a party piece, for lots of friends and family. Vary the ingredients as whim takes you: add different citrus elements; decorate with stripes or cross-hatching: it is an irresistible concept.

TO SERVE 16

ALMOND PASTE FILLING
750g (1lb 10oz) ground almonds

500g (4 cups) caster (superfine) sugar

1 teaspoon ground cinnamon or cassia, and extra for dusting (optional)

1 teaspoon gum mastic, crushed to a powder, (optional)

125ml (8 tablespoons) orange flower water

1 teaspoon rose water (optional)

25g (¼ cup) finely shredded zest of lemons and oranges, mixed

500g (1lb 2oz) large filo pastry sheets

150g (⅔ cup) unsalted butter, ghee or s'men, melted

2 egg whites, whisked, for sealing

2 egg yolks, beaten, to glaze

2 teaspoons orange flower water

sifted icing (confectioners') sugar, to decorate

1 Make the filling: combine the almonds, sugar, cinnamon, gum mastic, most of the orange flower water, all the rose water and the zests. Mix and knead these together to create a dense, flavourful paste. Roll this dryish mixture into 2cm (¾ in) thick 'sausages', each a little shorter than the length of the filo sheets.

2 Have the melted butter and a pastry brush nearby; the whites in a separate bowl; the yolks in a third bowl. Keep the filo covered using a tea towel or sheet of heavy plastic.

3 Set one filo sheet with its long side nearest you. Brush the sheet all over with some melted butter. Add a 'sausage' of the paste about 2cm (¾ in) in from the front edge; and 2cm (¾ in) shorter at one side.

4 Cover the almond filling with the front flap; roll it away from you. Slide it onto a buttered baking sheet. Use two hands to shape it into a tight curve, shuffling the filo pastry gently from both ends as you do it, to prevent tearing: a sort of concertina effect. Pinch closed the central curl. Curve the remainder tightly round it. Brush melted butter on top.

5 Repeat the process but this time to join the ends, brush the new piece of filled pastry with some egg white to help it bond, then slip it inside the other section. Continue the curving movement. Continue this shaping, curving. To each join add a little beaten egg white. Brush the butter on the top surfaces.

6 Finally the coil will end when all its filling runs out: pinch closed this end neatly. Brush the pastry all over with the egg yolks mixed with 2 teaspoons of orange flower water. Bake in an oven preheated to 170°C (325°F) for 40–45 minutes or until fragrant, browned and crunchy.

7 Serve warm, cool or cold (not ever chilled), dusted with sifted icing (confectioners') sugar with radiating lines of dusted cinnamon or cross hatching if liked. To serve, cut the 'snake' into tiny wedges: slide each portion out onto a serving plate, supporting it from beneath.

VARIATIONS

Use skinned, slivered pistachios, ground, instead of almonds. Experts suggest rose water is best to flavour this. Use a mixture of pinenuts, walnuts and almonds. Flavour using some dark rum. Knead minced lamb, golden raisins, cassia or cinnamon, allspice and parsley. Mix with half its volume of the sweet filling: excellent as a sort of westernized 'Christmas mincemeat' version of 'snake'.

ghoriba cookies

These easy but delicious little cookies are perfect after a meal, eaten between meals, or even eaten at breakfast with a cup of mint tea or fresh fruit juice.

MAKES 40–48

50g (¼ cup) ghee, unsalted butter or s'men
3 tablespoons extra-virgin olive oil
2 eggs
200g (1⅓ cup) icing (confectioners') sugar, sifted
400g (2½ cups) semolina flour (often sold as *semoule fine de blé*), sifted
1 teaspoon double acting baking powder, sifted
¼ teaspoon salt, sifted
2 teaspoons vanilla extract or orange flower water
50g (⅓ cup) extra icing (confectioners') sugar, sifted, for dusting
silicone paper, for cooking

1 Preheat the oven to 180°C (350°F). Heat the ghee and oil together until they mix.

2 Use a hand-held electric beater to whisk the eggs until frothy. Sieve in the icing (confectioners') sugar until fluffy, pouring in the ghee–oil mixture.

3 Stir in the dry ingredients, mixed, reduce the beater speed to slow, mix to a soft pliable dough. Add the vanilla extract. Beat briefly again. Divide the dough into 8 segments. Divide each segment into 5 or 6.

4 Using icing (confectioners') sugar-dusted palms, roll the balls to a smooth ball. Push each ball into the icing (confectioners') sugar. Pat to flatten slightly. Set each, sugared side up, on the silicone paper.

5 Bake for 15 to 16 minutes. Cool on the baking sheet. Dust all over with more icing (confectioners') sugar, if liked, and serve with mint teas, spicy coffee of other accompaniments of choice.

keneffa (pastry cream dessert)

I have enjoyed this elegant dessert at the *Maison d'Hôtes Riad Kniza*, in the Marrakesh Medina. It is somewhat like an Arabic version of *millefeuille* but has a surprise fragrance.

SERVES 4

6 ouarka sheets (*feuilles de brick*) or 6 filo pastry sheets
4cm (1½ in) depth virgin olive oil, for deep-frying
2 dried, scented pink rosebuds
1 tablespoon ground cinnamon or icing (confectioners') sugar

CUSTARD

8 tablespoons cornflour (cornstarch) or plain white flour
125g (generous ½ cup) white caster (superfine) sugar
50g (½ cup) ground almonds
1 litre (4½ cups) creamy milk
2 tablespoons rose water
1 teaspoon almond or vanilla extract
25g (2 tablespoons) butter

Illustrated on half title page.

1 Use a 12cm (5 in) metal cutter to produce 20 or 24 ouarka circles. Heat the oil to 180°C (350°F) and fry them, briefly, one by one until pale brown and crisp. Remove and drain on crumpled kitchen paper.

2 Make the custard: combine the cornflour (cornstarch), 100g (scant ½ cup) of the sugar and the ground almonds, stir in 250ml (generous 1 cup) of the milk to make a liaison. Keep aside.

3 Heat the remaining milk to near-boiling, then stir in the liaison; cook, stirring, over medium heat until thickened and reduced, 5–6 minutes.

4 Stir in the rose water, extract of choice and the butter. Stand the pan in iced water to cool, and leave until completely cold.

5 Grind the dried rosebuds with the remaining sugar to a powder using an electric spice grinder. Keep for decoration.

6 Set one pastry disc on each of 4 plates. Spoon a heaped tablespoon of custard onto each. Repeat this process until all the pastry is used up. Sprinkle some rosebud sugar on top, then create a pattern using cinnamon or icing (confectioners') sugar. Serve immediately.

Acknowledgements

A huge thank you to Helen Simpson and Annie Austin for their wisdom and local knowledge and for introducing me to Ahmed Nait Director of Travellink, Morocco whose expertise, generosity and altruism made my time in Morocco so remarkable. To his staff members, Khalida Hilm and Mustapha, my thanks.

Warmest gratitude to Prince Fabrizio Ruspoli of *La Maison Arabe* and his enlightened staff for their hospitality and stylish welcome.

The associated cookery school of *La Maison Arabe* was a delight and Mohammed Nahir very informative.

Mohammed and Kamal Bouskri of Riad Kniza showed me such kindness and epicurean fun.

To stallholders Lakrimi Mustapha and Jama: your herbs, spices and oils were a joy.

Finally: thank you to M. Ben-Harrou for your skills, and warmth and enthusiasm.